A TEACHER'S GUIDE TO

USING SCHOOL BUILDINGS

Sallie Purkis

English ⌗ Heritage

CONTENTS

TOP LEFT: From booklet accompanying radio broadcast for schools, 1933.
BOTTOM LEFT: Bedford Lodge Collegiate School for Girls, Clacton on Sea, Essex, 1907.
TOP RIGHT: Attendance certificate, Radford School, Warwickshire 1905.
BOTTOM RIGHT: Staff at Bergers School, London, 1930.

How Animals move on Land
By DORIS MACKINNON

GOING ON ALL FOURS

NEVER ABSENT   NEVER LATE

ROSS FROM RIVER.   E.S.A. LONDON.

Mike Corbishley

Norman Jacobs

Martin Nicholls

Mike Corbishley

ABOUT THIS BOOK

Every year schools all over the country research the history of their school. Many select a significant date in their history and mark it by an end of term exhibition or publication, using documentary and visual material collected from the County Record Office and the local community. Many start off knowing very little about historical methods and sources and with only a vague idea of where they are going but invariably end with a great sense of achievement about the discovery and recording of a history which has not been written down before. A common feeling at the end also is how enjoyable it has been for those involved.

This book is to help them and others embarking on a history of the school for the first time. Each section focuses on a particular line of enquiry. Different classes in the school could focus on one aspect initially and pool their work at the end of the project. Some schools may not feel that every line of enquiry is appropriate for their school and will select what they can reasonably attempt. It may be a beginning for a much larger project, which expands way beyond the initial objectives. There are also suggestions about what to do with the research, bearing in mind that teachers and students in the future may wish to take the project forward.

SCHOOLS AS HISTORIC MONUMENTS

The individual school history is a semi-private study. To the people who work or have worked there, to pupils past and present and to members of the local community who may have served as governors or benefactors, the building is a personal and private space. There is no where else quite like 'your' school.

However, schools are public institutions, funded by public money, administered in most cases by the County Council. Just as we

Impington Village College, Cambridge. Model of college built 1938-9.

place the building of cathedrals and castles within the historical context of the medieval period and learn something about building techniques, design, technology and the needs and values of the people of that time, so school buildings make statements about the period of time when most of them were built. As well as recording the material evidence in front of them, students can learn how to 'decode' or interpret it, thus gaining an insight into a methodology for looking at other kinds of building.

Schools, your own or others in the locality, are a prime example of the material culture of nineteenth and twentieth century Britain, both in terms of their form or design, the practical functional arrangement of the building and the changes that it has undergone during its lifetime. The design of schools often reflect the dominant views and values about the purpose and practice of education, which people held at the time. Additions to the building met different needs - increasing numbers of pupils within the catchment area, the admission of students of a different age or sex from that originally intended, changing ideas about the curriculum, demands for use of the building outside school hours, changes in technology to service the needs of those using the school. Each phase of a school building has an architectural message of its own and clues to be decoded, as changes to structure of the

building were paralleled by changes within and often, by working practices. Have you ever thought about the school building as:

- an example of a style or 'school' of architecture?

- part of the history of art and design?

- part of a national history of education, including a source for discussing how the curriculum has changed?

- a source of information about the history of building materials, techniques and technology?

- a series of clues about how buildings function, in terms of heating and sanitation arrangements?

- a building which conveys a statement about public values, civic pride, respect for learning, expectations about young people, standards of health, hygiene and safety?

- evidence of activities within the building, some involving small, some large groups of people?

- part of the history of the neighbourhood and how it has changed over time?

- part of the history of individual lives?

3

EDUCATIONAL POLICY AND SCHOOL BUILDINGS

School buildings are designed, built and modified as a result of laws passed through Parliament or policy decisions made by Local Education Authorities. So they can provide a lot of information about the history of education. Legislation has to be translated into brick, stone and concrete as well as into teaching methods. Changes of name, alterations to the original building and the allocation of space inside and outside alike provide clues about national education policy. Sometimes this reflects the aspirations and values of the period. But population changes and the amount of the national budget the government in power made available to education also influence what was built.

School Assembly hall at the turn of the century

Beamish Open Air Museum

KEY DATES

1801
Joseph Lancaster opens his free school in Southwark, using pupil-teachers. Soon afterwards he begins touring the country and raising subscriptions to found local schools.

1810-11
The Royal Lancasterian Institution (later the British and Foreign School Society) and the National Society for Promoting the Education of the Poor are set up to campaign for subsidies for education on behalf of Nonconformists and of Anglicans respectively. 'British Schools' and 'National Schools' begin to be built. Lancaster publishes *Hints for building, fitting up and arranging schoolroom*s.

1833
The first government grant for school-building voted by the Reform Parliament.

1839-40
The Committee of the Privy Council on Education is established and publishes model plans for schoolrooms.

1847-52
Campaigns by Church of England supporters to build schools in a strict Gothic style: e.g. Henry Kendall's *Designs for Schools and School Houses*, and the model designs for small rural schools and master's houses by William Butterfield published in *Instrumenta Ecclesiastica*. Committee of Council on Education produces influential new memorandum (1851) on school-planning.

1856
The Education Department replaces the Committee of the Privy Council on Education.

1870
W. E. Forster's Elementary Education Act leads to the setting-up of School Boards, charged with the task of providing non-denominational elementary schools for all in their area. Boards are quickly set up in English cities.

1874
E.R. Robson, architect to the London School Board, publishes *School Architecture*, with advice on the layout and style of board schools. After this date the so-called 'Queen Anne' style starts to supplant Gothic for schools in many cities.

LEFT: Woodwork room, Dunraven Secondary Modern School, London 1955.

RIGHT: Leeds Board School, c1900.

Mike Corbishley

Beamish Open Air Museum

1880s
Halls begin to be phased out for teaching in board schools and used mainly for assembly, dining and exercise in conjunction with adjacent classrooms. The first 'higher-grade' schools are built as an extension of the elementary system.

1889
Government subsidy allows county councils to pay for technical and higher education outside the board-school system. But evening schools begin to develop in urban board schools.

1899
The Board of Education is established, and the school-leaving age is raised to 11.

1902-3
The Balfour Acts controversially abolish School Boards. County and Borough Councils became responsible for the provision of schools, so that elementary and secondary education can be administered together.

1906-7
First official school meals and school medical service established. School plans henceforward must be approved by local Medical Officer of Health.

1918
School leaving age raised to 14. But average class size in elementary schools is 60 pupils.

1922
Labour Party pamphlet by R.H. Tawney called *Secondary Education for All* marks start of campaign to provide secondary school places for all children. But cuts in government spending curtail new school building.

1926
First 'Hadow Report' of the Consultative Committee to the Board of Education recommends national organisation of schooling into primary and secondary schools, with pupils transferring at the age of 11 after an examination. Under 'Hadow reorganization' many new secondary schools will be needed.

1931
Hadow Report on primary schools recommends separate buildings for infants and juniors. Board of Education publishes suggestions for planning secondary schools, encouraging specialist rooms, gymnasiums and playing fields around schools. Further spending cuts slow down school-building.

1936-9
'Mini-boom' in secondary school-building, slowed down by rearmament programme and ended by war.

1944
Butler Education Act establishes a Ministry of Education. Grammar, technical, modern or comprehensive schools are to be built for secondary pupils, depending on their differing abilities and the policy of the local education authority. Wood Report recommends light or prefabricated construction in post-war school-building.

1945-50
Rise in the birthrate at end of the Second World War. Estimates suggest that 200,000 new school places will be needed, particularly in the primary sector.

1947
School-leaving age is raised to 15. Primary school-building boom begins.

1949
Financial crisis causes Ministry of Education to publish new rules on cost and planning of schools.

1954
First purpose-built comprehensive school in England, for 2,000 girls, is opened at Kidbrooke, London.

1965
Comprehensive schools become official government policy; secondary modern schools are phased out. Some LEAs introduce First, Middle and High School pattern.

1966
School-leaving age is raised to sixteen. Government encourages growth of 'community education', so that adult facilities like swimming baths and libraries can be integrated with secondary schools.

1989
First City Technology College opened.

SCHOOL ARCHITECTURE

Earliest schools

The first schools were not purpose-built. They took place in any large room that was available. Schools were accommodated in refectories in monasteries, in barns or in houses. Pupils of all ages sat together in a single room. After the Reformation, Elizabethan and Jacobean benefactors often founded local grammar schools, which were originally simple buildings built in a plain Tudor style. When schools began to proliferate in the early nineteenth century, they were at first mostly funded by religious bodies. So architects often designed schools in the Gothic style traditional to English churches. This style was especially popular for Church of England schools between 1830 and 1880. When the School Boards were formed, Bradford, Birmingham and many other cities adopted Tudor or Gothic architecture for their earliest schools.

The Old Grammar School, Hawkshead, Lancashire. Endowed in 1575 but altered in subsequent centuries. William Wordsworh was a pupil here 1777-1783.

ABOVE: St Augustine's Church School, Pendlebury, Greater Manchester, built c1875.

BELOW: Wornington Road School, Kensington, London, built in 1873.

Tudor Features

■ **Square-headed windows with mullions and casement openings**

■ **Hood moulds over doors and windows**

■ **Low gables**

■ **Diapered brickwork**

Gothic Features

■ **Pointed arches**

■ **High and sharp gables and roofs**

■ **Narrow windows with pointed or cusped heads**

■ **Buttresses**

■ **Tall and prominent bellcotes or bell turrets**

■ **Chimneybreasts on external walls**

ABOVE: Stroud Green
School, Haringey,
London, built 1895-7.

RIGHT: King Edward VII
Grammar School,
Sheffield, built, 1837-40.

The Queen Anne style

Many of the board schools built
after 1870, particularly in London,
were designed in a newly-
fashionable style known as the
Queen Anne style. This was a
nickname for a style loosely
associated with buildings built long
before in the reign of Queen Anne.
It was popular because it was not
associated with any of the
churches, and was thought to have
a friendly look better suited for
children than the severity and
gloom of Gothic. It was first
popular in London, but widely
taken up in brick-built schools all
over the country after about 1880.

The Education Act of 1870
meant that many extra school
places had to be found, particularly
in the big cities. As the school
buildings often had to fit on to a
smallish plot of land, urban schools
at this time were often two or three
storeys high. This is how they were
described in a Sherlock Holmes
story by Arthur Conan Doyle
called *The Naval Treaty*:
'Look at those big isolated clumps
of buildings rising up above the
slates, like brick islands in a lead
coloured sea.'
'The Board Schools!'
'Lighthouses my boy, Beacons of
the future! Capsules with
hundreds of bright little seeds in
each, out of which will spring the
wiser, better England of our
future.'

Queen Anne Features

- Red brickwork, sometimes
  with terracotta ornament

- Prominent shaped or
  'Dutch' gables

- Large white-painted sash
  or centre-opening
  windows, allowing better
  light into schools.

- Decorative panels
  depicting flowers and
  plants or bearing
  the name of the school

The Neo-Georgian style

Georgian architecture is so named
because it flourished between 1714
and 1830, when four successive
English kings were called George.
It used features and proportions
used by the Ancient Greeks and
Romans for their grander buildings
and revived at the Renaissance.
The neo-Georgian style renewed
this tradition of building, following
the Gothic Revival interlude. The
ordinary brick houses of the
Georgian period were particularly
admired. Nearly all schools built
between 1900 and 1935 have some
of these features. This is how one
such school was described in 1911:
'The design is of eighteenth
century character, a fashion in

building which adapts itself readily
to modern requirements of light,
ventilation and arrangement and,
while of sufficient dignity, has a
domestic feeling which makes it
most suitable for school buildings.'
Many schools built between 1900
and 1935 were not in the centre of
cities, but in the suburbs where
land was available for playing
fields. The larger schools tended to
be lower and more spread out than
the old urban board schools.

Neo-Georgian Features

- Classical porches,
  entrances, columns and
  gates

- Regular, square-headed
  sash windows

- Parapets and pediments
  partly concealing the roof

- Symmetrical arrangement
  of classrooms behind a
  regular front with central
  entrance and wings

- Semi-covered walkways
  between different parts of
  the schools in the form of
  colonnades

The Modern Movement

Educational policy in the 1930s, particularly the attempts to reorganize the school system into infant, junior and secondary schools and to build schools more cheaply, offered new opportunities for architects. The changes also coincided with new architectural ideas which were coming to Britain from Europe and North America. The challenge was summed up in a book published in 1938, *The Design of Nursery and Elementary Schools.*

'Today all questions of school design are in an experimental and transitional stage. It is known that the compact, solidly-built, monumental school is unsuited to modern educational ideas, while the light, loosely grouped, flexible building is very suitable. It is also known that developments in the building industry are gradually making the latter type a more economical proposition.'

The full impact of these ideas was not felt until 1945, because the economic slump of the 1930s followed by the outbreak of the Second World War caused relatively few schools to be built

Modernist features

- Lots of glass in windows, sometimes covering one whole side of a classroom, to improve light for pupils

- Early metal window frames

- Flat roofs

- Doors opening from classrooms to the outside

- Landscaped gardens, with patios and plants

- Attempts to get away from a rigidly symmetrical pattern of planning schools

- Curving and other 'streamlined' features on staircase and ends of buildings

- Bigger and better lavatories, washing facilities and kitchens

TOP: Dartington School, Devon, Headmaster's house built in 1933.

ABOVE: Greenford County Secondary School, Ealing, London, built in 1938.

BELOW: Junior and Mixed Infants' School, Southall, London, built in 1937.

Andrew Saint

Andrew Saint

Andrew Saint

TOP: **Elliot School, Wandsworth, London built 1955-6.**
LEFT: **Aboyne Lodge Primary School, St. Albans, Hertfordshire, built 1949-50.**
RIGHT: **Hazelgrove Junior and Mixed Infant School, Hatfield, Hertfordshire, built in 1955.**

during these years. However, many schools built in the 1930s adopted a superficially modern look, while a few were fully designed according to the new principles.

Features of post-war schools

- Use of exposed steel and concrete

- Prefabricated panels and other building units

- Flat or gently pitched roofs

- Bold expanses of colour, inside and out

- Windows positioned to give a good quality of natural light, with views out as well as in

- Landscaping and tree planting schemes

- Informal, friendly planning, with larger secondary schools broken into many different units

Post-War schools

During the Second World War there were almost no new school buildings. But plans developed before the ending of hostilities promised not only new and better school buildings but a new system of education and the raising of the school leaving age. The baby boom of the late 1940s created an urgent need for school buildings, particularly on new housing estates. So the Government began to think how to plan and build schools quickly and by series rather than one by one, using new materials and prefabricated building methods. As much of the new schools as possible was made off site in factories, making them quicker and easier to assemble wherever they were needed. This explains why many post-war schools have features in common.

The buildings were individualized by means of variation in planning and layout, by gaily coloured tiled fascias and sometimes by specially commissioned works of art. Landscaping around schools also received attention. As time went on, classrooms ceased to be just well-lit square boxes off corridors, and secondary schools acquired many more specialized facilities. Educational reconstruction amounted to more than just the provision of new school buildings. Secondary education was reorganised first (in most places) on a selective system, later (again,

in most authorities) on comprehensive lines. These changes meant that large numbers of new buildings were needed, with each type of school - secondary modern, technical, grammar or comprehensive - having its own requirements. More schools were built in the twenty years after the Second World War and more teachers trained than at any other time in British history.

WARNING

Architectural clues can only tell you approximately the date of your school building. Remember that few people actually wear the latest fashion in clothes as soon as it appears and that the very latest styles are usually expensive. Since 1900, most school architects have been just as concerned with the inside of a school as with its design on the outside.

Two things have particularly influenced them:

- health, hygiene and light

- teaching style and classroom size

PLANNING YOUR PROJECT

A simple plan of action for a school building project might be:

- record the evidence (How do we know?)

- interpret the evidence (What does it tell us about the past?)

- communicate findings (What can we tell other people?)

- leave a record of our findings (What will people in the future want to know?)

TOP LEFT: Clacton School Board plaque, 1893.
TOP RIGHT: St Osyth Road Infant School. Boys' entrance, 1893.
BOTTOM RIGHT: St Osyth Road Infant School. Infants' and Girls' entrances, 1893.
LEFT: Greenside School, Hammersmith, London, built 1950-1.

Founder's memorial stone, St. Marylebone School, London.

LOOKING FOR CLUES

Look for clues in your building. Ask yourself why the building is arranged as it is. See if there is any connection between educational policy, government funding, ideas about the curriculum or teaching methods and the design of your building. Here are just a few clues to look for and some possible reasons for them. How many more can you find?

LOOKING AROUND OUTSIDE

What a building looks like from the outside is one of the clues which help to date it. Fashions in the design of buildings change over time, just like fashions in clothing. Sometimes the fashion, usually called a 'movement' in architecture, is for innovation; at other times copies of styles from

Clue	Possible explanation
Gates marked Girls and Boys	The sexes should be segregated at school
Ventilation Lantern on roof	To allow stale air out and fresh air in
Corridors	Public Health Regulations
Doors from classrooms to the outside	Design influenced by the 'Fresh Air' Movement
Central Hall	To allow an assembly of the whole school
Science Laboratories Economics Flat Gymnasium	Introduction of secondary education for all
School Kitchen	Provision of hot school meals
Open Plan Classrooms	Children allowed to move about. Team teaching.

the past are favoured. Examples of both can be seen when studying the architecture of school buildings. Some buildings have lots of clues about their architectural style; others just incorporate one or two aspects of the fashionable design of the time.

Many buildings also display a kind of 'body language' through their shape, size and external decoration, rather as people do when they dress up or stand or sit in a particular way. So think about the message the architect was trying to convey as you look at school buildings.

Form and Function
What a building looks like is only one part of an architect's job, particularly when designing a public building. Architects have to consider both form and function. They usually also have to work to a budget. At some periods in history more money has been made available for school buildings than at other times. So they cannot allow their imagination and

creative ideas to run riot.

Form involves thinking about the shape of a building, any decorative or ornamental features and consideration about how people will feel about it when they look at it, go into it and live in it.

Function involves designing a building that will work. Schools have to function for a lot of people and activities. There are the things needed by all human beings and things needed specifically for the building to function as a school.

Questions for discussion
What kind of features would be put into the form of building which was designed to impress people? What kind of design would make young people:

■ frightened and intimidated?

■ want to study as they entered the building?

Many old school buildings have a school bell in a bell tower or even a clock at the highest point of the building:

■ what message were they trying to convey to the pupils and their parents?

Make a list of all the things needed to make a school functional, eg heating.

Think about form and function when you look at the design of school buildings.

Look particularly at:

■ the skyline

■ the main entrance

■ the shapes used in the building

■ the decoration, including any lettering

■ how the building fits in with the other buildings around it.

BELOW: Roxeth School, Harrow, Middlesex built in 1851.

ACTIVITIES OUTSIDE

Random recording and the collection of miscellaneous information is not as efficient as recording for some purpose.
It is best to have some carefully-prepared objectives. This does not need to be a straight-jacket-type recording sheet with a series of tick boxes or closed questions; students will be motivated if they feel they have a job to do, not just filling in a form to please teacher.

More accurate data collection

Draw up a check list identifying some of the data that students can collect just from close observation of the building and its site.

■ What materials have been used in the building?

(How much brick. stone, wood, plaster, concrete, iron, slate, tile, asbestos, roofing felt, plastic, rolled steel, glass has been used?)

■ What evidence can you see from the outside about how the building works? Is there evidence of how it worked in the past?

(How many chimneys, flues, gutters, drains, entrances, exits, car parks are there?)

■ How big is it?

(How high, how long from end to end, how extensive is the school site? How many different ways of measuring can be thought of?)

■ What does it look like?

(What shapes have been used in the design? What colours? What decoration can be seen? How many people interviewed like the look of the building? How many dislike it?)

■ Was it all built at the same time?

(Are there additions to the original building? Is there evidence of change over time? Are there new entrances or exits? Has the original structure been modified or maintained?)

■ Is there evidence about the school in the form of writing or numerals?

(Where is the name of the school displayed? Is there any clear written information for visitors arriving for the first time? Are there older written clues on the stonework such as dates, foundation stones, entrances for boys, girls, seniors, juniors, infants?).

■ How can the school grounds be described?

(What details can be collected about fences, walls, gates, playground, playing fields, gardens, trees?)

Organising the class to collect data

Provide a variety of equipment and encourage pupils to select which is most suitable for their task.

Divide the class into small groups or pairs. Either give each group or pair a special responsibility for recording one aspect of the building or rotate the groups so that each starts at a different point. Emphasise that they are collecting information (evidence) about the school that might be used in a variety of ways. Some groups may choose to make a wall display or book; others may put their information on a computer database.

Role play

To emphasise the need for more accurate recording, the activity could be presented in the form of role play or simulation. In this case, each group would have to survey all aspects of the school building but from different viewpoints. This exercise will provide an opportunity for students to write in different forms of language for a specific audience.

☛ You are a team of County Council Surveyors and you have been asked to write a report on the structure of the school building and its grounds. There is an allocation in the budget for refurbishing the building and as it may be a long time before any more becomes available, you wish

DETECTIVE GAME

How well do you know your school building?

Arrange to have photographs taken showing some unusual shots of parts of the school building. Close-ups of details like door handles and window frames, which one normally takes for granted can be particularly puzzling when seen in isolation. Students should be asked to identify the feature, draw the area around the detail and say exactly where it can be found on the school building.

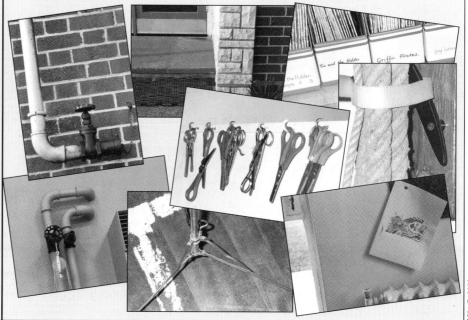

Mike Corbishley

to list not only those areas which need attention now but which may deteriorate over the next ten years. Do a systematic survey. You could start at one end of the site or at the top of the building and move down. You are only concerned with the outside on this occasion.

☞ You have been sent down from English Heritage. A new road is being planned and it has been suggested that your school should be listed as a building of historic importance, not necessarily because it is a very old building but because it represents a particular phase in school building over the last hundred years. Pictures or photographs should be included which show it off to advantage.

☞ You are a group of Travel Agents preparing the itinerary for a coach tour of your area for visitors from abroad. Your school will be one of the places they will see. Plan a brochure entry to describe it. Look at some commercial travel brochures and notice the particular kind of language they use.

☞ You have been asked to escort a group of partially-sighted students around your school and its grounds. You have visited an historic site where visitors may hire a Walkman and audiotour on tape. Prepare an audiotour for your school. Include a number of tactile experiences for the partially-sighted visitors.

☞ Your school is being put up for sale by auction. Students and staff will be relocated in another school. Prepare an estate agents' booklet, with photographs, presenting the school and its surroundings in the most favourable light you can. Select any parts of the building or site, which might be sold off separately (eg decorative doorways, sports pavilions etc)

LOOKING AROUND INSIDE

It is not always easy to look at a place you know well with analytical eyes. The inside of the school building however can provide clues about educational ideas which were current when the building was planned. Some of the original fixtures, fittings and

English Heritage

Classroom display. St Osyth Road Infants School.

decoration may well be intact and others, such as honours boards added. If educational policy has caused the school to change, for example from a single sex school to a co-educational one, from a secondary modern to an upper school, then the changes are likely to have necessitated changes to the structure of the building.

Looking for clues
An architect's plan will be helpful when investigating the inside of the school building and a walk round with an ex-teacher or ex-pupil with a tape-recorder will provide information about how the school has changed, carefully-focused observation will also yield results and probably be the easiest method to put into action.

Look for:

■ how the space has been allocated. What proportion has been given for classrooms where anything might be taught; what proportion to specialist accommodation?

■ the fixtures and fittings - lights, heating, door furniture, toilets and washbasins, gymnastics apparatus, a stage.

■ the decoration - this may include lettering styles as well as interior design features such as murals or tiling.

Health and Safety
Health and safety have always had to be major considerations for any school architect. The introduction of compulsory education at the end of the nineteenth century drew attention to the generally poor health of many families,

particularly in the large cities. As can be seen from many log book accounts, infections spread rapidly when large numbers came together in one place. Epidemics of diphtheria, measles and scarlet fever and old school photographs sometimes show children whose heads have been shaved because of headlice. After 1903, all designs of school buildings had to be approved by the County Medical Officer. This influenced a change in design from schools where all the classrooms were entered from a central hall to the 'pavilion' style, with corridors allowing for the frequent circulation of fresh air. The recommended method of interior decoration was ceramic tiling, which could be washed down when necessary. As the century progressed the 'Fresh Air' movement gained in influence; verandas and larger windows became popular, to allow natural light and sunshine into classrooms.

Control, discipline and teaching style.
The design of schools also reflects attitudes towards the control of pupils and how much freedom of movement they would be allowed. Some early classrooms were built on the 'gallery ' model. The desks were arranged in rows on steps, like the inside of a theatre or stadium. Large Board Schools were designed so that an experienced teacher could see into the next door classroom, where a more inexperienced teacher might be placed. Classrooms were often divided by partitions which could be rolled back so that two classes could be joined together.

More relaxed teaching styles have been in favour since the Second World War, particularly in primary schools, where teachers were expected to provide plenty of activity and experience for their pupils. Open-plan schools, where classrooms do not have dividing walls also favoured a team-teaching approach and many schools built in the 1960s and 1970s were designed so that each group of classrooms had its own facilities. Some older schools wishing to turn to modern and more open styles of teaching had walls and doors removed. Corridors, originally built as access routes and to allow for the circulation if fresh air, have also been used over time for different curricular activities. On some of the earliest school plans they are labelled as marching corridors. Children could be drilled, like soldiers, there or in the assembly hall. For many years they provided a space for coat hooks, but the modern tend is for coats to be put into cupboards and the corridors used as additional teaching spaces for small groups of children working on their or with an adult.

Making an impression

Most schools want to make a good first impression on those who come in either to work or as visitors. The school entrance may wish to give an impression of status and importance. Look for particular decorative features, such as coats of arms and honours boards. The school cups or other trophies may also be on display here. Some secondary schools have a war memorial showing the names of ex-pupils who were killed in one of the two world wars and information about how the money was raised for the memorial.

In the past extra money was often allocated for decoration of the entrance hall and assembly hall. Look for wood panelling, carving and other decoration that will not be evident elsewhere.

Many modern schools use their entrances and corridors to promote an impression of hard work and activity. Display boards have been put up to show off pupils' work or photographs of school events.

Heating, lighting and sanitation

There may be evidence in older schools of earlier forms of lighting and heating, such as where gas pipes once went up the walls, or where there were gas or early electric light fittings. All heating in schools was once coal-fired. Look for signs of how the school was heated before the present system was installed. Toilets, changing rooms and washing facilities are not always modernised as frequently as they should be. Look at the sizes of the fittings as well their shape, design and materials. Many school kitchens now look old-fashioned inside and may have changed from a place where hot meals were cooked to a place where frozen meals are warmed up.

Curriculum changes

The provision of space for specialised activities such as science, sport, home economics, art and craft was included in all secondary schools built between the wars and afterwards and the style of these facilities has changed very little. However, if your school once housed only boys and is now co-educational look for ways in which it was modified when the change occurred.

ACTIVITIES INSIDE

Interview an architect

■ If your school is less than 30 years old, one of the architects who worked on the design may well still be alive. Contact the County Architect's department.

■ Alternatively invite any architect into school to give an architect's view of the building.

■ Schools opened before the Second World War often had their opening reported in the local newspaper, which often mentioned the architect's name.

■ What questions would you like to ask the architect about the way the school was designed?

School guidebook

Look at examples of English Heritage guidebooks produced for historic sites and houses. Design one for your school which will appeal to one of the following groups:

■ new parents

■ new pupils

■ an inspector from English Heritage who is considering recommending that the school should be a 'listed' building.

■ the Old Students' Association who want to know how the school has changed.

Use drawings or photographs to illustrate the book and include interview material collected from pupils, teachers and other staff who work in the school.

BELOW: Sutton Primary School, c1900

Beamish Open Air Museum

Insulation survey

Your school governing body wishes to introduce an energy saving programme. Collect data on temperatures in different areas of the school and look for possible sources of heat loss. Make recommendations and estimate possible costs involved. Look at the following list of remedies which you may recommend.

■ Lowering ceilings

■ Fitting insulation panels

■ Double glazing

■ Replacing curtains

■ Fitting thermostats

■ Draught excluders

■ Sealing exit doors

AROUND THE SCHOOL BUILDINGS

Any study of the school building will be enhanced by consideration of the area surrounding the school. Why some schools have large playing fields and some have none is not just accidental. Like many aspects of a school study, this is a reflection of national policy and ideas about the purpose of education which prevailed when the school was built. Boundaries to the site and any deliberately-planned landscaping are also likely to have been the results of decision-making rather than chance.

The school yard

When the first schools were built with public funding, no-one really thought that the provision of any amenities, other than a school yard were necessary. In the large cities, hundreds of children had to be accommodated on a small site and schools with two or three storeys were commonplace. The school yard was surrounded by a high wall which emphasised the separation of school from home, the idea of compulsory education being something to which many Victorian parents and children took time to adjust.

Beamish Open Air Museum

Boy with bowler (hoop and stick), c1910.

Playing fields

The provision of sports fields and of access to the open countryside was part of the philosophy of the Hadow Report, which led to the establishment of separate primary (then called Elementary) and secondary schools. A pamphlet published by the Board of Education in 1931, *Suggestions for the Planning of New Buildings for Secondary Schools* was explicit about the choice of site.

'The site for a new school should be sunny, in an open situation and have no undesirable surroundings. It should be such that the necessary buildings can be suitably placed upon it, whilst leaving an area sufficiently level for use as playing fields. It should be conveniently accessible by road or rail so as to avoid unnecessary waste of time travelling. The entrance should not be on a main traffic route, but if possible on a side road leading off a main one. There should be convenient access from more than one side, but generally speaking, the less road frontage to the site the better. The most should be made of any natural advantages which the site may possess'

Much attention was focused on the teaching of P.E. in the ten years before the Second World War and a series of recommendations were issued by the Board of Education of the time about the quality of outdoor as well as indoor facilities.

Landscaping

In many rural schools and some urban, gardening was part of the curriculum but generally, landscaping was developed by architects, more for aesthetic than educational reasons. The introduction of modular building after the Second World War was not universally popular. Many complained about the visual uniformity and that it was impossible to distinguish one school from another. Ponds, shrubs and flower beds were therefore incorporated into plans to bring variety to the environment round the school.

Ordnance Survey maps

Discovering more about the site can be done easily by consulting an Ordnance Survey map produced before the school was built. In many cases it was farmland and some schools have even been named after the field on which the school was built.

Census returns and directories

Census returns and street directories, up to 1891, can be consulted in the County Record Office or Local Studies Library. These give information about every person living in a household, including scholars, so that any school which was built before 1891 will be able to find out the names of children living near the school, details about their families and parents' occupations. Although not as complete as census returns, street or county directories are available in libraries for periods later than 1891. They are another source for finding out exactly who lived in the houses near the school and what the householder did for a living.

Settlement patterns

There is a direct relationship between population shifts from one location to another and the need for a new school. New or revived industries create jobs; workers need houses and families need schools. Look for any correlation in your area between the age of local schools, the growth of housing estates and the rise and decline of local industries.

DOCUMENTARY EVIDENCE

GATHERING CLUES

Documents and personal memorabilia can confirm some of the assumptions made from looking at the building and may help to resolve some of the questions raised.

In the school cupboard

It is surprising how many documents which reveal information about the school's history remain in cupboards and on shelves. They should be listed and a copy of the list sent to the County Archivist for information. Look for some of the following in school:

- admission registers giving names, addresses and family details of past and present pupils

- punishment books

- architect's plans

- school log books.

Nineteenth century log books should not be retained in school. They are unique and valuable accounts and should rightly be deposited in the County Record Office, from where they can be borrowed. If they are kept in school, make sure they are properly housed in a fireproof cabinet

School photographs from the past frequently turn up in the backs of cupboards. These are likely to be of interest to people in the wider community and again, should be listed and stored carefully.

County Hall

At the office of the County Archivist or that of the County Architect, ask for any of the following:

- plans

- inventories of equipment in school. 1903 is a significant date because when responsibility

for schools passed from the School Boards to the County Council, most listed exactly what they now owned.

- surveyors' reports, again with 1903 a key date

- log books as mentioned above

- occasionally rarer items, sometimes regarded as ephemera, are found folded inside log books. These include copies of school rules and printed accounts, particularly where local people had been 'subscribers' to the school.

- school magazines

- newspaper cuttings.

Facsimile documents

Most County Record Offices do not have facilities for large groups of school children. Because of the interest in documents about schooling in the past, a number of County Councils have compiled packs of facsimile documents about education for classroom use. Some of these are listed in the bibliography, but enquire about what is available in your area from your own County Archivist.

Mike Corbishley

Information about school buildings may be collected from local newspapers.

Personal documents

While there may be some documents of a personal kind, which illustrate the individual experiences at school, in your County Record Office, you are most likely to recover these by a direct appeal to members of the local community by way of a letter home, a notice in the local newspaper or on local radio. You could ask for some of these:

- school photographs: those in private photograph albums may show a more informal side of school life than photographs taken for official purposes.

- school reports

- exercise and text books

- certificates for attendance, sport and other competitive events held at school

- programmes of concerts, open days and celebrations.

- gifts given to children at school: while these were often in the form of mugs to celebrate royal occasions, in some areas books or certificates were distributed instead.

**Records collected
from one family.**

Sallie Purkis

Admission No.	Date of Admission [or Re-Admission].			Date of Birth.			Surnames.	Christian Names.		Address.	What, if any, Claim to Exemption be made?
	Day.	Mon.	Year.	Day.	Mon.	Year.		Child's.	Parent's.		
1	15	1	1900	22	8	91	Furmidge	Harry Cyril	Henry	13. Rathmore Terrace.	No
2	"	"	"	19	3	89	Robinson	Georgiana	Edward	Blinco Grove.	No
3	"	"	"	18	10	87	Pluck	Lizzie.	William	" "	"

USING DOCUMENTS

Admission registers

Data about the pupils admitted to school in a particular term or month can be analysed. It can also be entered onto a computer database.

■ First names - comparison can then be made with the most popular names of children in the school now.

■ Surnames - members of the same family can be linked. A look through the registers for the years just before or just after the one selected for close analysis may well reveal other members of the same family and conclusions about family size can be drawn.

■ Age of pupils admitted. Has it changed in any way?

■ Catchment Area - a mapping exercise using a modern Ordnance survey map of the local area and one from the same period as the year chosen for analysis can be done showing where the pupils lived and how far or near the school it was. Comparison can be made with the addresses of present pupils. If the year chosen is before 1960 then pupils should consider how few would have come from car-owning families. How did pupils get to school?

This information may also be helpful when considering the probable date of the building of kitchens and canteens and could even lead on to an investigation of school transport provision over the years.

Architects' plans

Plans help understand what a building was like when it was first erected and how it has changed. Some plans include an elevation, the architect's drawing of what the school will look like when it is up. Some plans and elevations exist of buildings which were pulled down to make way for a new school. They can be used to reconstruct a day at school in the past even when very little other source material exists.

Plans as works of art

Early architects trained at colleges of art before the establishment of specialist schools or departments of architecture. Many architects plans are minor works of art, particularly the style of the lettering. This could be copied using steel nibbed pens dipped in ink, or fountain pens as an alternative.

Plan of primary school inside the grounds of Dover Castle, Kent, 1865.

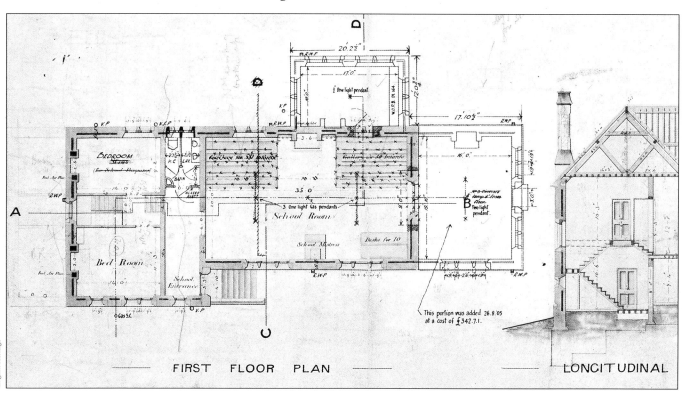

FIRST FLOOR PLAN   LONGITUDINAL

English Heritage

What to look for

■ Any details of the date when the plans were drawn and for whom. Terms like 'School Managers', 'the School Board' or 'X Borough Council' may help date them.

■ The number of storeys and how the upper levels were reached

■ The accommodation for teaching, including any indications of the use of space for specific activity or gender groups. Areas for large and small groups of people, including adults.

■ The size of each room

■ Lavatory accommodation and its location

■ Sources of water for washing or drinking. Kitchen or dining accommodation

■ Areas where heating fuel was stored. Information about boilers, fireplaces and flues.

■ Boundaries and entrances

■ Use of the area around the school

■ Any special architectural features such as a tower for the school bell or attempts at landscaping

Surveyors' reports and inventories

After 1903, most Local Education Authorities employed surveyors to make a record of the school buildings and their contents for which they were now responsible. These can be found bound in volumes, in alphabetical order, in most County Record Offices. Photocopies can easily be made for classroom use and they provide another opportunity to check on the appearance of the school building from the outside as well speculating on daily life within.

Great Oakley Primary School

4 July. Received Report of Scripture Examination:—
"Very fair throughout the school. — The school has undoubtedly suffered by the several changes which have taken place during this last year. We may with reason expect to find a good deal of progress at the next inspection. Many of the children's answers show mental laziness, while of course, every allowance must be made for really stupid children, the teachers should not allow any child to give less than his best thought.

Inspectors' report, 1917.

Schools for which no early plans are available can draw one of their own from detail contained in these surveyors' reports. Although the reports are dated 1903, they describe buildings unchanged since 1870 or before and list furniture and equipment that had almost certainly been installed when the school was first opened. Discussion of this will help students realise why historians have to question their sources and not accept what they read at face value. Surveyors' Reports can tell us:

■ size and inside appearance of the rooms

■ room contents, including furniture

■ facilities for heating, washing and the toilet.

Log books

The Principal Teacher must make at least once a week in the Log Book an entry which will specify ordinary progress, and other facts concerning the school or its teachers - such as the dates of withdrawal, commencements of duty, cautions, illnesses, etc - which may be require to be referred to at a future time, or may otherwise deserve to be recorded' Extract from the *New Code of Regulations* for 1872.

Log books were introduced as soon as substantial sums of public money were allocated to

Architectural terms used in old school plans	
Yard	Playground
Drill Yard	Space for children to be 'drilled', as in the army, an early form of P.E.
Offices	Lavatories
E. C.	Earth Closet (outside toilet)
Cloakroom	Place to hang hats and coats
Lobby	Porch or utility room
Gallery	A classroom built as steps, like the inside of a theatre, positioning all the children in view of the teacher.

schools. The intention was for them to provide a record which could be consulted by any authorised visitor to the school wishing to check on what went on there. They are a major resource for any study of education in the nineteenth and twentieth centuries and a particularly valuable and accessible source of evidence for students of all ages. Many log books remain in school cupboard, although, for safe keeping they should be deposited in the County Record Office where they may be consulted and extracts photocopied. They are hand-written, usually in a very clear style, bringing alive an almost domestic aspect of school life not only in the Victorian and Edwardian periods but up to the present day. They also provide details about the daily lives of real people connected with the school in the past - pupils, teachers, managers and visitors in a way that is rare in almost any other branch of historical enquiry. The obligation to fill in the log book has never been erased from the statute book and many heads continue to keep them today, though not in as much detail as their predecessors. A number of schools mark their significant anniversaries by publishing extracts from the log books.

Some of the information recorded in log books

- Names of staff and managers are listed both on appointment and when they resign

- Salaries paid to staff

- Names of individual pupils, particularly those responsible for deviant activities such as late arrival, truancy, misdemeanours

- Punishments

- Inspectors' Reports, often quoted in full

- Details of equipment and textbooks bought and introduced into the school. Lesson outlines.

- Programmes of school concerts and other entertainment

St Mary's Church School, Huntingfield, Suffolk

> ## List of Object lessons for Infants + Stan: I
>
> 1. A Brick.
> 2. A Book.
> 3. India-rubber ball.
> 4. A School slate.
> 5. A knife + fork.
> 16. Coal.
> 17. A barrel and a bucket.
> 18. A table.
> 19. A tallow-candle.
> 20. Leather.

ABOVE: Object lesson text from a school log book, 1898.
BELOW: Minute book entries.

Great Oakley Primary School.

> H.M. Inspector's Report for the year ending June 30th was read & much satisfaction was expressed at its terms.
> E.M. Britton who reached the age of 18 in Feb. last having received recognition as a supplementary Teacher (Art i of Code of 1909) — **1903**
>
> As regards 2. it was resolved to erect 2 wooden Earth closets in whichever of 2 sites might be recommended by the Committee of The DSC. — **1910**
>
> After some discussion it was decided that the bill for the Chimney & the repairing of the fences be left till after the Jumble Sale on Nov. 28 — **1932**

Activities using Log Book extracts

Looking Back Feature
Many local and national newspapers include extracts from their publications from the same day in the past. Collect some suitable 'Looking Back' items and publish them in the school newsletter.

Yearly Survey
Choose a particular week. Collect together significant items from the log book in that week over a period of time. Make an analysis of change and continuity over the period. Are there any connections between the activities of children in the past and those at school today?

Epidemic
Find an account of an epidemic in the school. Take on the role of the Medical Officer of Health. What makes you decide to close the school or to leave it open?

Lifelines
Draw a chronology of the events in the life of one of the headteachers who stayed at the school for some time. Beside it, record some of the major events which were happening elsewhere in the world at the same time. Compare the headteacher's experiences of life with someone famous who lived at the same time.

Boys and Girls
Compare entries which feature boys and male teachers and entries which feature females. Are there any differences?

Present Day
Keep a log book for your school for a time, adopting the style of the old one. Keep the entries short. How well do the entries reflect life at school today. List all the things that were not recorded in your log book because of the restrictions of space.

- Medical information about epidemics which closed schools and occasionally caused the death of pupils

- Information about holidays for harvests, fairs, national events

- Ways in which national and international events affected the routines of school life. For example when schools were evacuated or received evacuees.

- Comment on the weather, particularly when this was unseasonal and affected the school in terms of increased truancy, the need for more fuel etc

- Events and celebrations, such as Empire Day in the past, and school Sports Day in the present

- Records of pupils who pass examinations or win prizes

- Accounts of significant events in the life of the school, such as the opening of an extension or change of name.

Log book entries from the records of a primary school

School closes this afternoon, for organised picking of Blackberries, in accordance with Board of Education Circular 1056. — **1918**

Av. att. Mixed = 79.4   Infants = 30.1
Gerald + Joyce Gladwell, are excluded owing to Ringworm. — **1919**

Owing to parts of ceiling having given way, with consequent danger to children, school closes this afternoon, for repairs. — **1921**

Nurse Wallace called with reference to Dorothy Wrycraft, excluded on 3 March, verminous — still in the same state this morning — sent home by School Nurse, again. — **1922**

For dinner today only boiled potatoes + rice arrived. — **1944**

School did not meet today — being the occasion of the cessation of hostilities in Europe. — **1945**

Great Oakley Primary School.

PUNISHMENT BOOK

Year 1960

Date: Month & Day	Name of Scholar	Std. or Class	Nature of Offence	Punishment	Strokes	Signature (or Initials) of Teacher who Administered the Punishment
26/1/60	C. Gosling	3	Misbehaving - despite correction several times		3	P.P.L.
26/1/60	M. Prime	3	by boys' school staff.		3	
26/1/60	B. Harman	3	"		2	
26/1/60	C. Gosling	3	Deliberately breaking school rules.		2	J.DC
"	M. Prime	3			2	J.DC
"	B. Adrewar	3	" " "	" "	2	J.DC
26 Jan	R. Walker	2 B	Pricking boys with a sharpened stick during lesson		1	W.C.
28 Jan	J. Jones	1D(2)	Dangerous behaviour on the stairs		1	H.P.P.
28 Jan	G. Slattery	2B	Disobedience to (14)		1	W.A.I
2nd Feb	B. Wolfe	1 C	Sent out of class for insolence (14)		2	P.Ph.
3rd Feb	J. Jones	1d(2)	Misbehaviour in the dining hall		1	H.P.P
3rd Feb	C. Staver	1d(2)			1	H.P.P
4 Feb	J. Jones	1D(2)	Extremely bad behaviour for (9)		2	W.L.M.
15 Feb.	R. Corbyn	3	Damaging wall with lighted match (14)		2	N.L.M
17 Feb.	Watson	2B	Throwing a school text book in classroom. Administered by (14)		1	W.L.M.
2	B. Newman	3	Feet on desk / Talking whilst teacher was teaching		2	W.L.M.

Manor Community College

ORAL HISTORY

There are a number of good reasons why oral history is a popular and effective way of resourcing a schools project.

■ Reminiscences can help bring the history of a building alive.

■ Teachers and students can collect unique historical evidence that hasn't been retrieved before.

■ No special skills or expensive equipment are required. Good planning is the best recipe for success.

FINDING THE PEOPLE

It is tempting to restrict your interviews to individuals who were directly involved in your school building as pupils, teachers, managers or parents. However, before you begin consider whether there are enough people about able and willing to contribute. If you open up the project to include memories of schooling in general, it may enable more people to take part. In addition to gathering information about your school or others in the neighbourhood, there will be opportunities to contrast local experiences with those from other parts of the country or the world.

Decide who is going to conduct the interviews as they will need some very basic training, such as turning the tape recorder on and off and using a questionnaire. Video cameras can also be used to record oral history interviews.

Having made your key decision about the purpose behind your project, you will need to contact would-be respondents.

Design a handbill or press release

Whether it is done by hand, using only black and white, or word processed using a simple piece of desktop publishing software, the handbill will need to include the following information:

Oral history in action. INSET: a village school in the 1940s.

■ name of school and title of project

■ age and categories of local people you hope to interview

■ name and telephone number of person at school who can be contacted by volunteers

■ tear off slip which can be filled in by those who prefer not to use the telephone.

Circulate the request

Draw up a contact list which might include:

■ parents

■ grandparents

■ older neighbours known to the children

■ governors

■ former pupils, if there is a School Association

■ former teachers, known to the staff

■ organised groups of pensioners at clubs or in local sheltered housing

■ editor of the local newspaper offering it as a news item

■ local broadcasting station

■ local librarian who may put up a notice

■ doctors' surgery

■ local branch of Age Concern or Help the Aged.

The questionnaire

The questionnaire should include an opening question asking for the name of the respondent, when and where they went to school. Follow this with a series of open-ended questions, which will encourage the respondent to talk about their experiences at school, rather than provide answers on specific knowledge that could be discovered from other sources. Begin the tape by recording the name of the respondent, the names of the interviewers and the day's date.

Example of a questionnaire

The words in brackets are prompts, to jog the respondents memory when they are unsure about the purpose behind the question.

Memory Joggers

Not everyone has a good memory. If all the respondents have particular associations with your school, a special reminiscence box could be compiled containing objects, books, photographs and even recordings of familiar sounds like the school bell or school hymn.

A walk round the outside and inside the school is also a useful reminder. Carry a portable tape recorder to collect instant reminiscences.

Invite two people who were at school at the same time to come together. They will remind each other of what it was like in their time.

After the interview

Label and number each tape carefully, with the name of the person who was interviewed and the date on which the interview took place. Compile a card index or data base with as much detail as you can about the person on the tape. Oral history sources can be used in a number of ways both as transcribed extracts and as recordings.

Transcribed extracts

Write them in a book or album beside photographs of the school at the time and other historical source material such as extracts from the school log book.

Compare experiences

■ Memories of people who were at the same school at the same time.

■ Memories of people at different schools at the same time

■ Memories of school collected from different generations

■ Memories of school from those who were teachers and those who were pupils

Type the extracts and enlarge them on a photocopier. Draw pictures of the experiences described. Make a wall display and invite the respondents in to open the exhibition.

When and where did you go to school?
(first school, second school, third school, town, country)

What did the school look like from the outside?
(large school, small school, old, modern, architectural style, school grounds)

What was it like inside?
(old, modern, size of rooms, purpose of rooms, heating, lighting,)

Tell me about a typical day at school
(assembly, lessons, breaks, lunch, after school)

What did you learn there?
(3Rs, science, games, home economics, languages, art, music).

Were there different activities for boys and girls?

What did you wear to school?
(uniform, games, practical subjects, badges)

How were you expected to behave?

What happened if you didn't?
(school rules, manners, punishments and sanctions, rewards for good work and behaviour)

Were there clubs and activities outside school?
(after school, weekends, school trips, scouts, guides, CCF, sports)

Who were your special friends?

Which teachers do you remember?
(men, women, head, favourite subject)

Did you take any exams at school?

SCHOOL PHOTOGRAPHS

EARLY PHOTOGRAPHS

The building of the first Board Schools, in the 1870s, coincided with technical advances in the history of photography.

There are plenty of examples of early school photographs about and most Local Studies Libraries and County Record Offices can provide examples if you cannot find any for your particular school. Two styles of presentation were popular. In one, the class appears formally posed outside in the playground, with the teacher standing at the side. Sometimes the children are holding a blackboard giving the names of their form and year and occasionally a slogan is added such as 'Never Absent Never Late'. The other is an interior shot, which required more technical skill because of the light. The class have all been instructed to do the same thing, put their arms behind their backs or write on their slates. The photographs convey an atmosphere of good order and control. However, school photographs are more than just a record of a particular moment in time or historical examples of the development of photography. They provide evidence for many aspects of life in the past and can also be a source of information for role play and imaginative reconstruction.

Mike Corbishley

Beamish Open Air Museum

ABOVE: A woodwork room in the early 1920s.
RIGHT: Barnard Castle School, c1900.
BELOW: Crawford Street School, Camberwell, London, 1906. 'Legs astride, arms upwards bend.'

Greater London Record Office

Whole school photograph, Brentwood County High School, 1951.

Sallie Purkis

Gwyneth Mortlock

1936

1949

Gwyneth Mortlock

1954

Mike Corbishley

Tamara & Heather Corbishley

1992

Hannah Corbishley

1990

Questions

- What age do you think they are?

- Where was it taken?

- Do you think it was taken in summer or winter?

- How long ago was it taken?

- What did teachers and pupils wear to school then?

- Do you think they dressed up to have the photo taken?

- Why do you think it was taken?

- Why has it survived?

- Can you see any other clues about school life in this photo?

- Look at the expressions on the faces of the children and teachers.

- What words would you use to describe their feelings?

- Which person in the photo would you like to be?

- Which person would you not like to be?

- What do you think happened before this photograph was taken?

- What do you think happened afterwards?

- How does the photograph compare with a photograph of your form now?

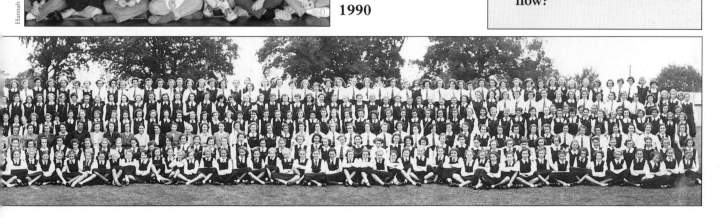

ANALYSING A COLLECTION

More photographs of your school will be in private photo collections than in the record office or library, although for publicity photographs (see below) your local newspaper archives should be contacted. Make an appeal through local networks to borrow as many as possible for your project. Try to make arrangements to have these photos copied so that the school will have a permanent collection.

The following list shows some of the categories of photograph that may be found.

■ **Formal group** photographs, of classes, of teams and of the whole school. The latter became popular from the late 1930s onwards when early movie-type cameras enabled a whole school to be recorded in one shot.

■ **Publicity photographs.** These were taken to show off particular aspects of the school curriculum and the facilities within the school to support it. Pictures of science laboratories, domestic science flats, gymnasia and woodwork rooms come into this category. They were often commissioned by Local Authorities, particularly to show off their new secondary schools and were often published in the press.

■ **Event photographs.** Public events such as the opening or closure of the school, the opening of an extension to the building, anniversaries, speech days, pageants and plays are usually photographed by the local newspaper. However there are also photographs of more private events such as the retirement of members of staff who have been at the school for a long time. Many of these are in private albums.

■ **Informal photographs** taken by members of the school. These include groups of friends, particularly on school trips or outings. When publicising a request for the loan of school photographs it is worth mentioning early movie films. Some geography departments

1954

1951

c1880

1952

1973

THE OLD LABORATORY IN GILBERD HOUSE

c1906

Mike Corbishley

1951

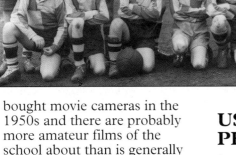

Norman Jacobs

2468

1923

Bernard Corbishley

1957

Photograph Record Form

Photo Number and brief title

Sepia /Black and White / Colour

Where obtained

Any information given by donor

Names of any people recognised in photo

Details of their dress, including school uniform

Why taken

When taken

Where taken

Photographer, if known

Any interesting detail not recorded above

bought movie cameras in the 1950s and there are probably more amateur films of the school about than is generally realised. These can now be transferred to video.

Keeping a record of your school photographs

When, as a result of your appeal, former pupils and teachers come forward with photographs, they should be invited to talk about them, the people in the photograph and the circumstances when it was taken. The information should be stored with the photograph. Each photograph collected should be allocated a number and entered on a Photograph Record Form. The data could also be put onto a computer database if preferred.

USING PHOTOGRAPHS

Chronology

Put the photographs in a time sequence. Try to borrow some old cameras or pictures of cameras which could have been used to take the photos. Put everything on display as though in a gallery and write a catalogue commenting on the changes in the development of photography as well as what can be seen in the photos.

Points of view

Write a commentary from the point of view of the photographer and from some of the people in the photographs.

Design a calendar

You have been asked to select photographs for a school calendar which will be sold for school funds. Choose photographs which fit each month of the year.

Then and now

Take some photographs at the same location as the old photographs. How has the background changed?

Strike a pose

Take a photograph of a group today, posed like people in the old photograph. Describe what it felt like.

SCHOOL OBJECTS

Objects used at school are further evidence for changes in education over time. Many remain in the school building, either still in use or in storage. Museums have collections of artefacts, many small objects, such as school badges, remain in private hands and it is not unusual to find old textbooks in charity shops or at jumble sales. Photographs, pictures and inventories provide more evidence about the material culture of school life.

FURNITURE

The introduction of compulsory education created a demand for the mass production of school furniture and a number of specialist firms, such as E J Arnold at Leeds, began life at this time. Many patented their designs, using such names as 'The Imperial' and marketed them though catalogues. Architects have also influenced the design of movable furniture in schools as well as the fixtures and fittings.

School desks

Many people reminiscing about their school days vividly recall the discomfort the experienced getting in and out of two and three seater desks with fixed backs, something which modern children experience when they go to spend a 'Victorian' school day in a museum re-enactment. Their design suggests a style of teaching and classroom management where control and instruction dominated. Teachers, if they sat down, had high chairs so that they could see everyone at the same time. Designs were not significantly changed until the 1930s when the expansion of secondary education meant that benches and tables replaced desks in some specialist areas such as laboratories, housecraft rooms and art studios. As the curriculum on offer widened so individual desks, each with its own storage space or 'locker' were introduced into many classrooms.

Beamish Open Air Museum

TOP LEFT: **Registration board.**
TOP CENTRE: **Teacher's seat from a 1901 catalogue.**
TOP RIGHT: **Single desk from a 1901 catalogue.**
LEFT: **Beamish School, 1913.**

In the postwar period, the use of lightweight tables in primary schools became widespread as methods of teaching shifted from an instructional model to an activity model, with an emphasis on collaborative learning and group work. Equipment was stored in sliding trays around the classroom and tables could be used flexibly according to the activity.

Graffiti

Old school desks are sometimes a source of unofficial communication about the lives of previous incumbents. Their own names, the names of those they admire or comments on their experience as reluctant learners are all very common expressions of the art.

School cupboards

Cupboards remain in schools far longer than desks and a search will probably reveal one or two that have been there since the school was first opened. Using a framework of questions, similar to that suggested in *A Teacher's Guide to Learning from Objects.* (English Heritage, 1990), will enable students to look more closely at the cupboard as an historic object, to record details about it for the

school record and to use the information to make comparisons with other furniture in the school.

Physical features

■ Material used, including type of wood if known

■ Surface treatment, paint, varnish

■ Current condition

■ Evidence of any alterations over time

■ Size, including inside layout

Construction

■ Number and size of pieces of wood used

■ Types of joints

■ Method of closure, including observation of any change over time

Function

■ Size of shelves or space inside

- Any writing clues, eg labels on shelves

- Has it always stood in the same place?

- Comparison with more modern storage units

- Could it be used elsewhere eg a home, an office

Design

- Design clues which relate to function e.g. glass doors

- Decoration

Value

- Is it still useful in school or is it really just an interesting bygone?

- Value as a historical source. What does it tell us about school in the past?

- Commercial value to an antique dealer

TEACHING AND LEARNING AIDS

Equipment used in schools in the present and in the past also provide information about what subjects are taught in school and what teaching methods are used to help children learn.

Equipment used in Victorian schools has now often been moved to a museum and is available either as part of a Victorian school day or in a museum loan box.

You may be able to borrow some items from the following list:

- abacus, for helping infants learn to count and calculate

- slate and slate pencil (replicas also available)

- various kinds of pen - quill, dip, fountain

- containers for ink

- globes

- maps and charts for hanging on the wall

BELOW: Double desk with slates from a 1901 catalogue.
BELOW RIGHT: Inkwell holder and slates.

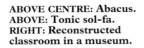

ABOVE CENTRE: Abacus.
ABOVE: Tonic sol-fa.
RIGHT: Reconstructed classroom in a museum.

- dumb bells, used in early forms of gymnastics

- textbooks, often inscribed with the name of the school

- copybooks which taught children to write (replicas available)

- rarer items include a box which contained samples of natural materials like wool, cotton and coal which teachers used for Object lessons, an early form of science teaching

- many Victorian log books contain entries which mention teaching aids used in school.

Mike Corbishley

Attendance and conduct medals.

Audio-visual aids
From the 1930s, when the provision of electricity became standard, at least in new schools, more sophisticated audio-visual aids were employed. Many of have since become obsolete and overtaken by technological, but are not as sufficiently valued for their historical interest as Victorian teaching aids. It is possible that some lie in the backs of cupboards at your school and should be recovered as an example of teaching methods at a particular point of time in your school's history. Such equipment would be useful as a memory jogger for a retired teacher who would be able to recall the lessons taught using such aids.

SHIELDS, CUPS, MEDALS AND PRIZES
Competition has long been a feature of British education, starting with the School Boards in the 1870s.

Attendance prizes
Regular attendance at school was one of the first achievements to be publicly recognised in the form of school medals or elaborate certificates. Book prizes were also given, usually inscribed with a commemorative label, something which Sunday Schools did throughout the nineteenth century.

Competitive sport
Organised competitive sport first became widespread in the 1870s as well, with the foundation of the

Football Association, numerous sports tournaments and events. The public schools took up team sports as part of their ethos, competing with each other for inter-school trophies, a practice which was adopted by all state secondary schools who could acquire the necessary outdoor space. Sports fields were also included for as many primary schools as possible after 1945.

The design of sports shields and trophies emphasises the importance the donors placed on the activities. Some examples made before the Second World war are minor works of art with fine metal working and engraving. The presentation of sports trophies, to individuals or teams,is nearly always an event which has been photographed, often for the local newspaper. Winning a prize or trophy is something which people remember and can be asked about in an oral history interview.

Academic prizes
Prize Days, when books were presented for academic success, became a fixture in the school year of most secondary schools. Old copies of school magazines are a good source to investigate and lines of enquiry could focus on purpose of each prize as well as on the names of the recipients.

BADGES AND UNIFORM
Responsibility within school as prefects or monitors was usually signified by the presentation of a badge of office. The badge was handed back to the school, when the recipient's term of office

ceased. As these badges were so small, many will be lost, but an appeal may find some. A few even turn up in flea markets and when examined will be seen to be excellent examples of inter-war enamelling techniques.

Cloth badges for sewing on to school uniform are another source. Each school had its own criteria for offering these as rewards.

School uniform
No other country adopted school uniform with the enthusiasm of the British. The practice originated with the charity schools, who clothed their poor scholars as well as educating them. Pupils at Christ's Hospital and other similar charity foundation schools still wear the sixteenth century uniform of their first scholars. Like competitive sport the uniform tradition began in the nineteenth century public schools and was taken up enthusiastically by grammar schools and secondary schools, until many people believed that to have a uniform at all was a mark of a good school. Clothing manufacturers and shops competed for the large market which compulsory uniform provided and their catalogues show the range of items which became available. Cash's woven name tapes also became established as a result of the demand for identical school uniform.

While each school prided itself that its uniform was unique and made its students look distinctive beside other schools, each item was only a variation of a standard pattern. Uniform also has special vocabulary of its own.

Our popular modern Gym Tunic

G943. *On right.* Made from all-wool serge that is soft-handling, yet hard-wearing and guaranteed fast colour. Perfectly cut, made and finished. Modern round-neck, flared style with zip side opening; concealed pocket in side of skirt and a lined back panel to prevent seating. A 3-in. hem for lengthening and a clever 1¼-in. turning at the waist line allow for extra bodice length and future adjustment of the waist line. In navy only. Note the very keen prices !

| Lengths | 24-26 | 28-30 | 32-34 | 36-38 | 40-42 ins. |
| Prices | 47/6 | 52/6 | 57/6 | 62/6 | 67/6 |

G915. *Not illustrated.* The classic pleated style with square neck. In all-wool serge with self-lined yoke. Pocket in side seam. Has 3-in. hem and a 1½-in. let-down at shoulder. Navy only.

| Lengths | 24-26 | 28-30 | 32-34 | 36-38 | 40-42 ins. |
| Prices | 45/- | 52/6 | 60/- | 67/6 | 75/- |

GRAND RAINCOATS
at economical prices !

G590. *On left.* A real triumph of quality and value. Tailored with great skill from a gaberdine cloth of selected Botany wool and pure Egyptian cotton. Proofed to withstand all but exceptional conditions. Fully lined with additional protective interlining at all vulnerable points. 'Captive' belt, 3-in. turnings to sleeves and hem. In navy.

G578. A serviceable and well-cut raincoat in union gaberdine. For the more slender budget. In navy.

Lengths	24-26	28-30	32-34	36-38	40-42	44-46 ins.
G590	110/-	120/-	130/-	140/-	150/-	160/-
G578	77/6	87/6	97/6	107/6	117/6	127/6

Green and brown raincoats are also available in our showrooms.

School Blouses

F7. Clydella blouse. Washes and wears splendidly. Cream only. Chest (of girl).

| 24 | 26 | 28 | 30 | 32 | 34 | 36 ins. |
| 16/6 | 17/6 | 18/6 | 19/6 | 21/6 | 22/6 | 23/6 | 24/6 |

F20. Poplin blouse cut and tailored to perfection with close-fitting cuffs and a trim collar that 'stays put.' White only. Chest (of girl)

| 24 | 26 | 28 | 30 | 32 | 34 | 36 | 38 ins. |
| 14/6 | 16/- | 17/6 | 19/- | 20/6 | 22/- | 23/6 | 25/- |

Sallie Purkis

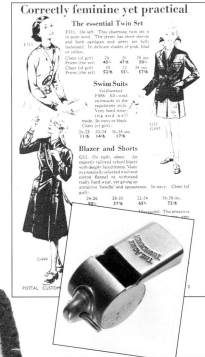

Correctly feminine yet practical

The essential Twin Set

F311. *On left.* This charming twin set is in pure wool. The jersey has short sleeves and both cardigan and jersey are fully fashioned. In delicate shades of pink, blue or yellow.

Chest (of girl)	24	26	28 ins.
Prices (the set)	45/-	47/6	50/-
Chest (of girl)	30	32	34 ins.
Prices (the set)	52/6	55/-	57/6

Swim Suits
Not illustrated

F588. All-wool swimsuits in the regulation style. Very hard wearing and well made. In navy or black. Chest (of girl)

| 26-28 | 30-34 | 36-38 ins. |
| 11/6 | 14/6 | 17/6 |

Blazer and Shorts

G11. *On right, above.* An expertly tailored school blazer with deeply faced fronts. Made in a specially selected wool and cotton flannel to withstand really hard wear, yet giving an attractive 'handle' and appearance. In navy. Chest (of girl):

| 24-26 | 28-30 | 32-34 | 36-38 ins. |
| 50/- | 57/6 | 65/- | 72/6 |

Macgoshel. The attractive ... grey

POSTAL CUSTOM

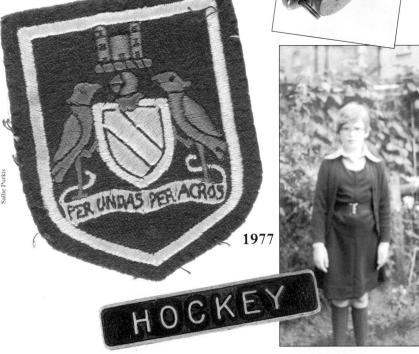

1977

Helen Norman

Sallie Purkis

- Skirts and trousers: grey or black trousers for boys. There have been more changes in the requirements for girls than for boys. 1900 - 1940: gymslips, sometimes called tunics in navy maroon, bottle green or grey. Divided skirts for games. 1940- : skirts for girls usually grey, navy, maroon or bottle green. The introduction of trousers for girls was only achieved in many schools after considerable pressure from girls, women teachers and mothers. They are still disallowed, illegally, in some schools.

- Shirts and ties: uniform for both sexes.

- Blazers: for both sexes. Additions to the standard blazer in the form of braid and badges usually signified status.

- School bags: these deserve an investigation as an item that has changed over time. School satchels used to be standard for both boys and girls but bags carried to school now vary according to the current street fashion.

Questions for discussion
List as many arguments as you can which people may have used in the past for having a distinctive school uniform?

- What arguments would opponents of school uniform have used?

- Is there an unofficial uniform among students at your school today?

- Make a survey of the most popular garments worn. Are any garments or fashions specifically banned? Why?

- Should sports continue to have a place at school or should they be an extra- curricular activity?

A VICTORIAN SCHOOL DAY

A number of museums and Local Education Authorities have facilities which enable children to have a living history experience as pupils at school in the Victorian period. However, many schools organise their own, particularly if they are celebrating an anniversary or moving to a new site.

Pupils from Lowbrook Primary School, Maidenhead taking part in a Victorian school day at Katesgrove Schoolroom.

PREPARATION

Clothing

■ Boys: white shirt, waistcoat or jacket, peaked cap, trousers tucked in socks.

■ Girls: dark dress or calf length dark skirt and white blouse, black tights or knee length dark socks, lace up boots or shoes, white pinafore or smock (easily made from rectangle shape). Long hair plaited.

■ Teachers:
male: dark trousers, jacket and white shirt, moustache.
female: dark skirt, black tights, lace up boot or shoes, highnecked white blouse with brooch, hair in a bun.

Classroom
Reduce the size of large windows by using large sheets of sugar paper. Cut 'Gothic' window shapes in the paper. Arrange desks in rows, with blackboard (and easel if available) at front. Decorate sheets of paper as proverbs with a moral message and hang on walls, eg

■ God is Love

■ Waste Not Want Not

■ Look Before You Leap

■ More Haste Less Speed

■ Rich Is He That Is Content

■ Idleness Rusts The Mind

Add a picture of Queen Victoria. Bring in oil lamps, if available.

Equipment

■ Slates: if slates cannot be borrowed or bought, black sugar paper or hardboard painted black is an acceptable substitute.

■ Globe

■ Long stick to be used as pointer for blackboard or wall charts

■ Handbell to signify start and finish of lessons

■ Sheets from a copybook

■ Dip pens and ink (if available)

■ Hymn sheet with words of *All Things Bright and Beautiful*

■ Chart showing multiplication tables to be chanted in unison

ON THE DAY
Line children up in playground with boys and girls using separate entrances.

■ Inspect finger nails

■ Any lessons which introduce rote learning or repetition of information given by teacher

from front of class

■ Copy book writing

■ Hymn singing

■ Bible reading

■ Drill, either in classroom or playground

■ Sewing - buttonholes, darning or samplers

■ Playtime - hopscotch and other traditional games rather than football

Diversion
If possible arrange for a 'visitor' to the school or an 'incident' which the children are not expecting. The visitor could be the vicar, his wife and daughters or a school inspector. The school log book is certain to have a record of an actual visit or incident which took place.

FOLLOW-UP
Discussion after the event, out of role, can focus on comparisons between now and then, the sources used by teachers to plan the day, feelings about the teaching and control methods used and views about the school day as may have been held by pupils, teachers and visitors.

SCHOOLS ACROSS THE CURRICULUM

A project based on your school will provide many opportunities for developing skills, knowledge and understanding in most areas of the National Curriculum.

HISTORY

The history of the school fits into the Programmes of Study at Key Stages 1 and 2. Through school buildings, your own or other in the locality, you can introduce KS1 children to a time both 'within and beyond' living memory. At Key Stages 2 and 3 it could be included in a local history study. The historical sources of buildings, sites, adults talking about their past, photographs, artefacts and documents, which are listed in the National Curriculum Programmes of Study, are all relevant aspects of a school history investigation. Activities can focus on various levels of attainment and involve children in making deductions from historical sources, raising questions and showing understanding of change and difference. Many school buildings were altered as a result of parliamentary legislation and Victorian school days and museum reconstructions of Victorian classrooms are good examples of 'interpretations of history'.

GEOGRAPHY

Drawing or using maps and plans of the school site will develop geographical skills and vocabulary. The relationship of the school to the area around it now and in the past can be built up by the use of old as well as modern maps. Journeys to school, routeways in and around the schools can be mapped or a trail of school and grounds prepared. Schools exist because of the houses and families who live near them. Old registers will show where the children lived and a comparison can be made with the modern catchment area. Older schools will almost certainly be built from locally obtained building materials, particularly in limestone areas. The schools in the area and when they were built will be a very important part of any locality.

SCIENCE

The brickwork or stonework can be monitored for signs of weathering. The ecology of the school grounds and surroundings, even in urban areas, can be investigated and recorded. Many schools use part of the school grounds as nature conservation areas. Keep a record of birds, insects and plants over a number of years so that successive generations can monitor any changes. A survey of doors and windows and how they open and close will help children understand forces and levers.

Beamish School (c1913) living history.

MATHS

Most dimensions of the school can be measured using equipment like trundle wheels and clinometers and the measurements converted into a scale so that a plan or elevation can be drawn. Scale models cross the boundaries between maths and technology. The importance of shape, angles and tessellation to a builder or architect will be understood in the context of a real building such as the school, particularly in the prefabricated school buildings from the post-war period. With budgets now a major feature of school management, practical examples of pricing, fundraising and allocating money can be used, rather than pages of money sums in textbooks. Calibrated timelines, with key events in the history of the school, or the date when all the schools in the area were built will improve understanding of how we measure historic time.

ART

The school building or parts of it can be reproduced in a range of media from pencil drawings, pastel, chalk and charcoal, prints, paintings and clay reliefs. Younger children can take rubbings of the bricks or stonework to develop understanding of texture. Decoration was a feature of the design and style of many older school buildings and some have lettering cut into stonework. Photography projects train children to look at small details and familiar things from new angles. The photographs and drawings can be used to design Christmas cards, embellish the school brochure or newsletters as well as going on display in the school itself. Sketches can also be the starting point for elaborate projects in embroidery, collage and friezes.

TECHNOLOGY

The school is a series of systems such as water systems, heating systems and electricity circuits. It is also a space for living and working and old buildings do not always meet the requirements of modern life. How has the building had to be adapted in response to changes in the curriculum? Scale models of the school, or parts of it can be built, and the design features of entrances, walkways and stairways examined in relation to the building techniques needed to erect them. Technology projects can include such things as designing a new school badge or logo for a particular occasion and designing and printing T-shirts and sweatshirts. Studying old photographs of the school can lead to an interest in old cameras and how they worked.

ENGLISH

Most aspects of English can be taught using the school buildings as a starting point. Oral history interviews involve children in the design of questionnaires as well as speaking and listening. Log books and other documents are also good examples of handwriting styles, such as copperplate, italic and 'Marion Richardson' which was popular in the 1930s. The history of the school can be presented as an exercise in sequencing; incidents from the past discovered through sources such as the log book or oral history can be written as newspaper reports. Information about school history projects need to be published in local newspapers and local radio as well as in newsletters to parents if people are to come forward with their memories and memorabilia. Since the time of Thomas Arnold and Charles Dickens, school has been a popular subject for writers of novels and poetry. A display of old annuals like 'School Friend' or school stories from Angela Brazil onwards would be interesting. School life today is also a good starting point for creative story and poetry writing as the children start with a familiar context.

CROSS CURRICULAR THEMES

Multicultural Education

The experience of going to school is common across all cultures and in all countries of the world today. Asking parents and grandparents for their memories of school, wherever it was, will produce a rich variety of experiences. What common themes, such as how teachers kept discipline, can be drawn out from them? In Victorian times, schools usually celebrated Empire Day on 24 May. Look for reports in school log books. Discuss the British Empire and how Victorian children were taught about it, using evidence from old globes, maps and hymns sung at school as well as log books and oral history.

Health Education

Log books also contain information about epidemics at school in the past of illnesses like diphtheria, scarlet fever, measles

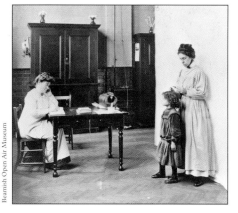

School clinic c1900

and chicken pox. In Victorian times children died from these diseases. How have they been virtually eradicated today? Look at arrangements for cleanliness and sanitation in the school building both now and in the past using either the evidence in the building or old plans. List all the design features which allowed children access to fresh air and sunshine.

Equal Opportunities

The history of education shows how attitudes have changed about the educational opportunities open to both boys and girls. Look for any evidence in the school site of separate entrances for boys and girls. Use old timetables to find evidence for boys' games and girls' games and of the class being divided for certain crafts like woodwork or needlework. Ask retired teachers about these situations in oral history interviews.

Economic Awareness

Make a study of how the school is financed. Make comparisons between funding today and funding in the past, for example by using school log books for evidence of any 'payment by results'. Ask teacher governors about the role of the governing body in the management of the school budget. Find out how much money the PTA contributes to the school and what it is spent on.

Environmental Awareness

Should old schools be pulled down or conserved as historical monuments? What is a listed building? Should your school qualify either now or in the future? If your school is near a main road, invite an environmental health officer into school to discuss any possible pollution from noise and petrol.

Citizenship

Find out about how people are elected to the County Council and what effect their views have on the management of your school. Invite school governors and question them about their responsibilities. How are elections to the PTA conducted? How are parents or teachers elected to the governing body?

BELOW: St Osyth Road School relay team, 1924.

BIBLIOGRAPHY & RESOURCES

School Architecture

McClure, S, **Educational Development and School Building, 1945-1973**, Longman, 1984. ISBN 0-582-03296-2.

Ringshall R, Miles M, Kelsall F, **The Urban School: Buildings for Education in London 1870-1980**, Architectural Press, 1983. ISBN 0-81539-695-X.

Robson, E R, **School Architecture** (1874), reprinted with an introduction by Malcolm Seabourne, Leicester University Press, 1972. ISBN 0-7185-5018-8.

Saint, A, **Towards a Social Architecture: The role of school building in Post-War England**, Yale University Press, 1987. ISBN 0-300-03830-5.

Seabourne, M, **The English School: Its Architecture and Organisation 1370-1870**, Routledge and Kegan Paul, 1971. ISBN 0-7100-6882-4.

Seabourne M, and Lowe R, **The English School: Its Architecture and Organisation 1870-1970**, Routledge and Kegan Paul, 1977. ISBN 0-7100-8408-0.

Ward, C, **British School Buildings: Designs and Appraisals 1964-74**, The Architectural Press, 1976. ISBN 0-85139-085-4.

The History of Education

Avery, G, **The Best Type of Girl: A History of Girls' Independent Schools**, Andre Deutsch, 1990. ISBN 0-233-98642-1.

Davidson A, **Blazers, Badges and Boaters: A Pictorial History of School Uniform**, Scope Books, 1990. ISBN 0-9066-1925-4.

Frankum, W and Lawrie, J, **The Victorian Schoolday: A Teachers' Manual and Resource Folder**, 1992. Available from Katesgrove Schoolroom (see Museums listing).

Hurt, J S, **Elementary Schooling and the Working Class 1800-1918**, Routledge and Kegan Paul, 1979. **ISBN 0-7100-0275-0.**

McClure, S, **A History of Education in London**, Penguin, 1990. ISBN 0-7139-9034-1.

Martin, C, **A Short History of English Schools**, Wayland, 1979. ISBN 0-85340-669-3

Parsons, C, **Schools in an Urban Community: A Study of Carbrook, 1870-1965**, Routledge and Kegan Paul, 1978. ISBN 0-7100-8986.

Silver, P & H, **The Education of the Poor: The History of a National School 1824-1974**, Routledge and Kegan Paul, 1974. ISBN 0-7100-7804-8.

Victorians at School, a Teachers' Pack from Ironbridge Gorge Museum Trust, Telford, Shropshire, 1992.

The History of Childhood

Adams, C, **Ordinary Lives a Hundred Years Ago**, Virago, 1982. ISBN 0-86068-239-0.

Burnett, J, **Destiny Obscure: Autobiographies of Childhood, Education and the Family from the 1820s to the present day**, Allen Lane, Penguin, 1982. ISBN 0-1400-7345-0.

Horn, P, **The Victorian Country Child**, Alan Sutton, 1985. ISBN 0-86299-157-9.

Humphries, S, **A Century of Childhood**, Joanna Mack and Rob Perks, Sidgwick and Jackson, 1989. ISBN 0-2839-9756-7.

Humphries, S, **Hooligans or Rebels?** Blackwell, 1982. ISBN 0-6311-3286-4.

Thompson, T, **Edwardian Childhoods**, Routledge and Kegan Paul, 1981. ISBN 0-7100-0676-4.

Fiction and semi-fiction which incorporates autobiographical material

Bronte, C, **Jane Eyre**, Blackie Nelson, 1980. ISBN 0-2169-0939-2 (first published 1847).

Hughes, T, **Tom Brown's School Days**, Puffin, 1983. ISBN 0-1403-50225 (first published 1857).

Lee, L, **Cider with Rosie**, Penguin, 1962. ISBN 0-1400-1682-1 (first published 1959).

Lawrence, D H, **The Rainbow**, Penguin, 1949. ISBN 0-1400-0692-3 (first published 1915).

Thompson F, **Lark Rise to Candleford**, Penguin, 1973. ISBN 0-1400-3672-5 (originally published 1939-1943 as three titles).

Articles

Aldrich R, **The History of Education in Schools**, Teaching History 39, 8-10, 1984.

Crimp L, **The Old School**, Remnants 7, English Heritage, 1989.

Eddershaw, D, **Period Classroom Re-Creations**, JEM 11,29-32, 1990.

Educational approaches

Copeland, T, **A Teacher's Guide to Geography and the Historic Environment**, English Heritage, 1993. ISBN 1-85074-332-0.

Durbin, G, Morris S and Wilkinson S, **A Teachers Guide to Learning from Objects**, English Heritage, 1990. ISBN 1-85074-259-6.

Keith, C, **A Teacher's Guide to Using Listed Buildings**, English Heritage, 1991. ISBN 1-85074-297-9.

Education packs

Dodwell, F, **Hitchin British Schools: A History of the Buildings**, North Hertfordshire District Council, 1990.

Dodwell, F, **Hitchin British Schools: Schooldays 1810-1900**, North Hertfordshire District Council, 1993.

Johnson, S and Leslie, K, **Schools and Slates: Sussex Schools in the 1880s**, West Sussex Records Office.

Going to School in Victorian Times, Hampshire Records Office Education Service.

Good Morning Children, Age Exchange Reminiscence Centre, London.

Could do Better, Children at School 1870-1925, Charlotte Mason College and Cumbria Archive Service, 1990.

Books for children

Clarke, A, **Finding out about Victorian Schools**, Batsford, 1983. ISBN 0-7134-3667-0.

Dures, A, **Schools**, Batsford, 1971. ISBN 0-7134-1772-2.

Martin, C, **Schools in History**, Wayland, 1984.
ISBN 0-85078-456-5.

Marshall, P, **School Days: A History in Photographs**, 1850 to the present day, Macdonald, 1984. ISBN 0-356-10144-4.

Mountfield, P, **Women and Education**, Wayland, 1990.
ISBN 1-852-10-647-6.

Purkis, S, **At School in 1900**, Longman, 1981.
ISBN 0-582-18434-7.

Purkis, S, **At School in the 1950s**, Longman, 1983.
ISBN 0-582-18783-4.

Purkis, S, **Exploring Schools**, Wayland, 1988. ISBN 1-85210-301-9.

Ross, A, **Going to School**, A and C Black, 1982.
ISBN 0-7136-2240-7.

Speed, P F, **Learning and Teaching in Victorian Times**, Longman, 1964. ISBN 0-5822-2107-2.

MUSEUMS

Reconstructed classrooms with living history facilities

The Board Schoolroom,
Bradford Industrial Museum and Horses at Work,
Moorside Road,
Eccleshill, Bradford, BD2 3HP
0274-631756

Katesgrove Primary School,
Dorothy Street,
Reading, RG1 2NL
0734-574678

Centre for Environmental Education
Great North Road,
Stibbington,
Peterborough, PE8 6LP
0780-782386

Wigan Pier Heritage Centre,
Wigan, WN3 4EU
0942-323666

Fringford Old School,
Oxfordshire County Museum Service, Fletcher's House,
Woodstock, Oxfordshire, OX71SN
0993-811456

The Commandery Civil War Centre, Sidbury, Worcester,
WR1 2HU
0905-355071

The Ragged School Museum Trust,
46-48 Copperfield Road,
London, E3 4RR
081-980 6405

Museum of Childhood,
Judges' Lodgings,
Lancaster, LA1 1YS
0524-32808

Merseyside Museum of Labour History,
Merseyside Maritime Museum,
Albert Dock, Liverpool, L3 4AA
051-207 0001

Schoolrooms reconstructed within museums

North of England Open Air Museum,
Beamish, Co. Durham, DH9 0RG
0207-231811

Weald and Downland Open Air Museum, Singleton,
Nr. Chichester, West Sussex,
PO18 0EU
0243-63348

Dewsbury Museum,
Crow Nest Park,
Heckmondwike Road,
Dewsbury, WF13 2SA
0924-468171

The Living History Centre,
Herdings School,
Norton Avenue, Sheffield,
S14 1SL
0742-653273

Staffordshire County Museum,
Shugborough,
Milford, Stafford, ST17 0XB
0889-881388

Sevington School Project,
Sevington, Chippenham,
Wiltshire, SN14 7LD
0249-783070

Museum of Childhood,
Sudbury Hall, Sudbury,
Ashbourne, Derbyshire, DE6 5HT
0283-585305

Warwickshire County Museums Service, St John's House Museum,
St John's, Warwick, CV34 4NF
0926-412021

Museum of the History of Education,
Parkinson Court, The University Leeds, LS2 9JT
0532-334665

Museum of London,
London Wall, London,
EC2Y 5HN
071-600 3699

Museum of East Anglia Rural Life,
Abbot's Hall, Stowmarket,
Suffolk, IP14 1DL
0449-612229

Acknowledgements
The author and editor gratefully acknowledges contributions received from the following people: Rosie Barker, John Benoke, Celia Clark, Chris Forster, Wyn Frankum, Hilary Goldson, Heather Harrison, Liz Hunter, Norman Jacobs, Julie Jordan, Jo Lawrie, Stuart Leach, Martin Nicholls, Andrew Saint, Maggie Samuelson, Jennifer Smith, Helen Thompson, Pat Yates. A particular thanks to is due to staff and pupils at Great Oakley C of E school, Essex, Ms L Trotter, staff and pupils at St Osyth Road Infants School, Clacton.